TRADITIONS AND CELEBRATIONS

VAISAKHI

by Anita Ganeri

PEBBLE
a capstone imprint

Published by Pebble, an imprint of Capstone
1710 Roe Crest Drive, North Mankato, Minnesota 56003
capstonepub.com

Copyright © 2026 by Capstone. All rights reserved. No part of this publication may be reproduced in whole or in part, or stored in a retrieval system, or transmitted in any form or by any means, electronic, mechanical, photocopying, recording, or otherwise, without written permission of the publisher.

Library of Congress Cataloging-in-Publication Data is available on the Library of Congress website.

ISBN: 9798875219979 (hardcover)
ISBN: 9798875219924 (paperback)
ISBN: 9798875219931 (ebook PDF)

Summary: Vaisakhi is a spring harvest festival and the Sikh new year. On this important holiday, Sikhs celebrate the founding of their community, the Khalsa, by Guru Gobind Singh. Wearing their most colorful clothes, they listen to holy readings and welcome new people to the faith. Sikhs share a big meal with people of all faiths. Many attend exciting parades with music, sword-fighting displays, and singing. Lively photos and easy-to-read text help readers learn about contemporary celebrations of this community-focused holiday. Readers will discover how the Sikh community celebrates its history with joy and generosity.

Editorial Credits
Editor: Kellie M. Hultgren; Designer: Elijah Blue; Media Researcher: Rebekah Hubstenberger; Production Specialist: Tori Abraham

Image Credits
Alamy: Art Directors & TRIP, 13, Dinodia Photos, 9, Michael Wheatley, 28, Pacific Press Media Production Corp., 6, Well/BOT, 14; Getty Images: Carl Court, 1, Chip Somodevilla, 17, Dinodia Photo, 24, iStock/HarjeetSinghNarang, 27; Shutterstock: AbhishekMittal, 22, betto Rodrigues, 5, ChiccoDodiFC, cover, 21, explorewithinfo, 11, Loredana Sangiuliano, 23, Marygrace_97, 19, OlegD, 18, Skyshark Media, 20, zixia, 16

Design Elements
Shutterstock: Rafal Kulik

All internet sites appearing in back matter were available and accurate when this book was sent to press.

TABLE OF CONTENTS

What Is Vaisakhi? 4
The Story of Vaisakhi 8
Vaisakhi Celebrations 16
More Vaisakhi Customs 26
    Glossary 30
    Read More 31
    Internet Sites 31
    Index 32
    About the Author 32

Words in **bold** are in the glossary.

What Is Vaisakhi?

Today is Vaisakhi, the happiest festival of the Sikh year. It falls on April 13 or 14.

For weeks, Sikhs have been busy getting ready for this special day. They cook delicious food, practice songs and dances, and make costumes.

Everyone is welcome to join in. You do not have to be a Sikh. Sikhs believe in treating everyone as equal. They want to share their love for their faith.

A Vaisakhi parade

For Sikhs, Vaisakhi is the start of a new year. It happens during the spring harvest. Farmers bring in their crops. They say prayers for a good harvest next year.

On Vaisakhi, Sikhs also remember an important day in their history. It is the day the Khalsa began. The Khalsa is a **community** of Sikhs who **dedicate** their lives to their faith.

The Story of Vaisakhi

Sikhism began in the **Punjab** hundreds of years ago. In 1699, **Guru** Gobind Singh was the leader of the Sikhs. At Vaisakhi, he called all the Sikhs together. They came from all over the Punjab.

The Sikhs crowded outside Guru Gobind Singh's tent. They were ready to celebrate. But when the Guru came out, he had a sharp sword in his hand. He asked if anybody was willing to die for their faith. Nobody answered. They were too scared.

Guru Gobind Singh

The Guru asked again. A brave young man called Daya Ram answered. The Guru led him into his tent. A few minutes later, the Guru came out again. He was alone. His sword was covered in blood.

The Guru asked again and again. Four more Sikhs came forward. One by one, he led them into his tent. Each time he came out alone, holding his sword.

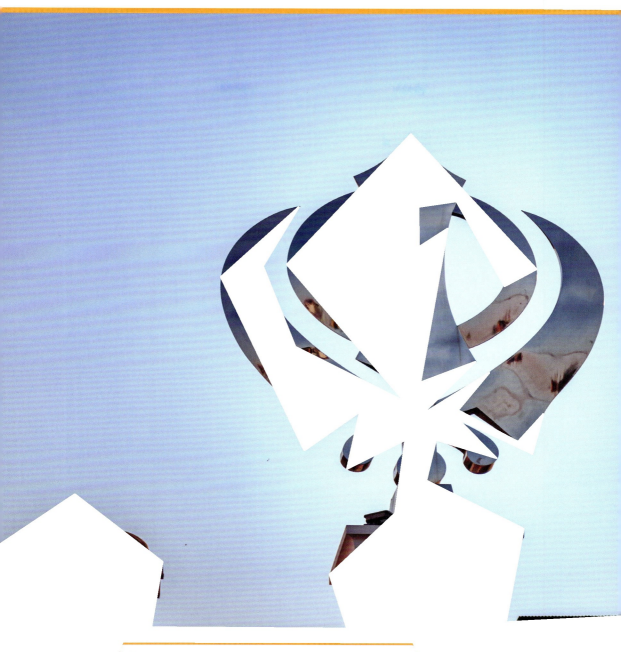

The Khanda is the symbol of the Sikh faith. The symbol has a sword at its center.

People were getting worried. Where had the five men gone? What had happened to them? They were afraid that the men were dead.

Then an amazing thing happened. Guru Gobind Singh came out of his tent, leading the men behind him. They were dressed in bright orange and blue clothes, like the Guru. They were all alive and well!

The Guru told the crowd that these men had been very brave. They proved their love for their faith.

A painting of Guru Gobind Singh and the five faithful men outside the tent

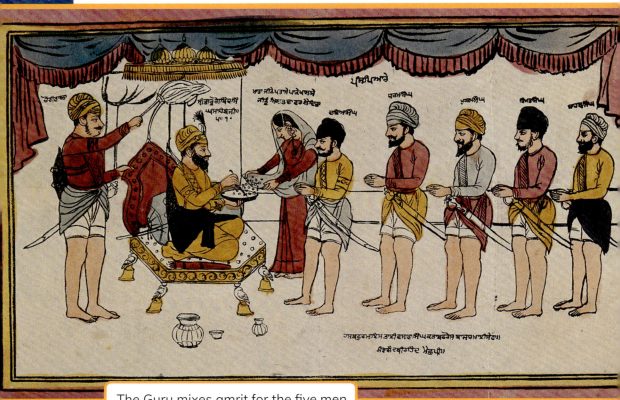

The Guru mixes amrit for the five men.

Then, Guru Gobind Singh **baptized** the men. They became the first members of the Khalsa. He called them the Panj Piare. This means "Beloved Five" in the Punjabi language.

The Guru said prayers. He prepared a bowl of **amrit**. He stirred it with a sword. He gave the five men some of the amrit to drink. He sprinkled some of it over their eyes and hair. This marked the start of their new lives in the Khalsa.

Vaisakhi Celebrations

Today, at Vaisakhi, Sikhs remember the five brave men. They come together to celebrate their faith. The day starts with a visit to the **gurdwara**. This is a building where Sikhs meet to worship.

Sikhs gather for Vaisakhi in a gurdwara.

In the gurdwara, worshippers say prayers and sing **hymns**. They listen to talks. People read from the *Guru Granth Sahib*. This is the Sikh holy book.

Like the Panj Piare, many young Sikhs join the Khalsa at Vaisakhi. They put on orange and blue robes. They wear the Five Ks that show their faith. They let their hair grow long and wrap it in a **turban**. They wear a wooden comb, a metal bracelet, and white shorts. They carry a small knife. They go to the gurdwara for the amrit ceremony.

The Five Ks

Kesh: uncut hair

Kangha: a wooden comb

Kara: a metal bracelet

Kachera: white shorts

Kirpan: a small dagger

A kirpan

Afterward, the celebrations begin. Crowds of people line the streets, waiting for the Vaisakhi parade. The banging of drums gets louder and louder. The parade is nearly there!

Five Sikhs lead the parade. They are dressed like the Panj Piare. They hold swords or orange and blue Sikh flags. A brightly decorated **float** follows them. It carries a copy of the *Guru Granth Sahib* in a place of honor.

Hundreds or even thousands of people follow the float. They wear traditional clothes in bright colors. They sing hymns from the holy book. Some dance a traditional dance called **bhangra**. The beat of the drums keeps them in time.

Bhangra dancers

A girl displays gatka.

People display gatka, an Indian martial art. Fighters use wooden sticks instead of swords. They slash and spin. They have to be quick on their feet!

People eat langar at a gurdwara in India.

Sharing food is very important for Sikhs. It shows that everyone is equal. And it is a way of helping others. At the gurdwara, people take turns to cook and serve a meal every day. It is called **langar**. It is free for everyone to enjoy. And at Vaisakhi, it is especially busy!

By evening, everyone is hungry. It is time for a Vaisakhi feast. Family and friends gather at home. They eat spicy chickpea curry, lentil dal, samosas, and Indian sweets. Delicious!

More Vaisakhi Customs

Sikhs celebrate Vaisakhi all over India, but especially in the Punjab. Many people travel to the city of Anandpur Sahib. This is where Guru Gobind Singh lived. The Khalsa began there.

A gurdwara marks the spot where the Guru baptized the Panj Piare. At Vaisakhi, it is decorated with flags and twinkling lights. Crowds of people go there to worship.

The Takht Kesgarh Sahib Gurdwara in Anandpur Sahib

The Vaisakhi parade in Surrey, Canada

The biggest Vaisakhi parade outside India takes place in the city of Surrey in Canada. Around half a million people take part in the parade. They come from all over Canada and the United States. They watch fabulous floats and dazzling displays. Sikhs serve free food and drink for everyone.

Vaisakhi is a joyful day when Sikhs share their faith with everyone. Happy Vaisakhi to all!

GLOSSARY

amrit (AM-ruht)—Sikh holy water made from water and sugar

baptize (BAP-tyz)—officially make a member of a faith

bhangra (BAN-gruh)—a style of music and dance from the Punjab

community (com-YOU-ni-tee)—a group of people who share interests and beliefs

dedicate (DED-ih-kate)—give all of your time and energy to something

float (FLOHT)—a large decorated vehicle used for festivals

gurdwara (guh-ruh-DWAA-ruh)—a building where Sikhs meet to worship

guru (GUH-roo)—a Sikh or Hindu religious leader

hymn (HIM)—a holy song

langar (LAN-guh)—a meal served at a Sikh gurdwara

Punjab (pun-JAAB)—a part of northwest India and Pakistan

Sikhism (SEEK-is-um)—the religion of the Sikhs

turban (TER-bun)—a long cloth that is wrapped around the head

READ MORE

Bradley, Fleur. *My Life as a Sikh: How the World Worships*. Ann Arbor, MI: Cherry Lake Publishing, 2022.

Kaur, Jasneet. *Sikh Festivals and Traditions*. North Mankato, MN: Capstone, 2025.

Kaur, Jasneet. *We Gather at a Sikh Gurdwara: A Place in Our Community*. North Mankato, MN: Capstone, 2026.

INTERNET SITES

Britannica Kids: Sikhism
britannica.com/topic/Sikhism

CBC Kids: Let's Celebrate Vaisakhi
cbc.ca/kids/articles/whats-the-story-vaisakhi

Little Sikhs: Vaisakhi
littlesikhs.com/vaisakhi

INDEX

amrits, 14, 15, 18
baptisms, 15, 26
Five Ks, 18, 19
foods, 4, 24, 25, 29
gatka, 23
gurdwaras, 16, 17, 18, 24, 25, 26, 27
Guru Gobind Singh, 8, 9, 10, 12, 13, 14, 15, 26

Guru Granth Sahib, 17, 21
harvest, 7
Khalsa, 7, 15, 18, 26
Panj Piare, 15, 18, 21, 26
parades, 5, 20, 21, 28, 29
Punjab, 8, 26

ABOUT THE AUTHOR

Anita Ganeri is an award-winning author of nonfiction for children. Born in India, she was educated at Cambridge University and has written more than 500 books, including the best-selling Horrible Geography series. She writes widely on the religion and culture of India and South Asia. Anita lives in the north of England with her husband, children, and rescued pets.